The Exiled Child
(2nd Edition)

Andre Andres X

ISBN: 979-8-9868641-0-5

About the Book

Author Andre Andres X's debut book, *The Exiled Child*, is the culmination of years of poetry. The book is split into three sections. The first part focuses on Black history and the Black experience in the United States. The second part is an introspection in which Andre ponders the purpose of life and his struggles with mental health. The third part is a small section about love.

The Exiled Child is an unapologetically Black work of art that is made for other exiled children, Black people, the children of the diaspora. Author Andre hopes that others can read his work and relate to the message in some of the poems.

About the Author

The author was born as Elgin Andres Woodard but prefers to go by his given name, Andre Andres X. He is from a small town south of Houston, Texas. Andre is a graduate from Houston Baptist University; it was there that his love for poetry began. He wrote a short poetry series inspired by the works of Langston Hughes for a college project, which was so successful that after graduation, he continued to write as a form of expression. Andre considers himself and his work to be revolutionary, and he is proud to be Black. Andre is someone who loves history and is unafraid to speak his mind; both of these characteristics can be seen in his art. Aside from writing poetry, Andre also has a podcast, *The X-Communicated*, available on all platforms, and he does photography that he posts on his social media.

Dedication

To the Ancestors.

To those who came before.

To those who didn't make it.

To those who guide us.

TABLE OF CONTENTS

Part One

A Black Life

Introduction

Critical race theory (CRT) will no longer be taught in schools; white children will learn even less about the crimes white people committed in this country, in history, against us. Black children will continue to be fed lies at school and hard truths at home. While white kids have been and will continue to be sheltered, every Black child's rite of passage is "the talk."

"The talk" is done to save our lives; it's a matter of survival. We learn about white people and what they're capable of. The inescapable truth of racism and discrimination in this country is taught at a very young age. The burden of this knowledge is crushing and traumatic. This fear is instilled in us, but this heartbreaking reality must be taught in order to preserve or at least extend this Black child's life...hopefully.

White people try to white out their crimes and prevent these things from being taught. So in my unapologetically Black work, I scream it. I'm not going to let them forget what they've done. I'm going to talk about it; I'm going to teach it; I'm going to share that knowledge. We owe it to the victims to remember them and not forget what they've endured. What we continue to endure.

I am The X-Communicated, it is an activist/artist name I gave myself in the legacy of Malcolm X. As The X-Communicated, I speak the hard, ugly truths because I want America to look at itself in the mirror. We still go through these things to this day.

I refuse to bring children into this world the way it is now; I don't have it in me to give "the talk" to my own children. I can't look those children in their beautiful brown eyes and tell them that the world hates them. That the world will try to destroy them, tear them down, and that they will have to face what their forefathers faced, as if a generational curse that we didn't deserve had been placed upon us. I don't have the heart to tell a child of mine that they'll have to work hard in life, twice as hard, to make it. I don't want to give them "the talk" that was given to me, and the one that was given to my father by his father, and my grandfather from his father, and so on.

I'm saying it all and holding nothing back. Some of these poems were painful to write. Tears were shed. I've mourned our Ancestors in some of these poems.

I remember when I was reading through the complete works of Langston Hughes when I first started working on my short five-poem series. I noted how some of the poems about injustice were so painfully relevant to today that if I were to simply change the date, you'd think it was written yesterday. It really puts things into perspective when you think about it. A poem written seventy years ago highlights the exact same violence we face today. I sincerely hope that anyone reading this collection of poems fifty years from now will not find them relevant. I hope by then it will simply serve as a history lesson of what was endured and a testament to some great change that occurred.

Black people have experienced 600 years of white supremacy. If we include the Arab slave trade, then we're talking over 1,000 years of Black oppression, longer than the millennium reign of Christ in the book of Revelation.

With this in mind, I know it'll take more than one summer of protests for change. It'll take longer than our lifetimes. It hurts me to say that I'm afraid these poems will still reflect the times fifty years from now. These poems will still be quoted to explain the problems of that generation. I pray to the Ancestors that I'm wrong. I hope I'm wrong.

You'll also notice in this section that some of the poems use religious elements. My degree is in Christianity, I do not believe anymore, but I still like to use some of the themes in my writing. The poetry varies in style from standard rhyme, spoken word, and song/rap form. I listened to a lot of protest music from the 60s and 70s while I was writing. Music such as Marvin Gaye's "What's Going On?" and Gil Scott-Heron's "Pieces of a Man" were albums that inspired some of my writing. I can't say that my poetry is a celebration, I mostly vented my frustrations. I like to call it "protest poetry."

For this edition of *The Exiled Child* I've decided to add some of my photo concepts to the book as well. At the end of the book I decided to include a section where I explain my inspiration for writing some of the poems. Art is up for interpretation so I won't be explaining the poems, just what inspired me to write them. My poems themselves tend to be pretty political and straightforward, so I won't be adding my political essays to the end of the book as I originally intended for this edition. However, I did add a few bullet points. If you want to hear more, then you can listen to my podcast, *The X-Communicated*.

THE EXILED CHILD

Mother, I know it is from you that I came,

So please answer this: What is my true name?

I have not known since the world united to tear you apart[1]

And they snatched your Black children and broke your heart.

Look at me, Mother; in your arms I did not grow.

I've been gone too long, and your rivers I'll never know.[2]

They sold us away to work and toil

On some strange and unsullied soil.

I lost my culture in those 400 years,

And each generation had struggles and tears.

Taken to a foreign land by foreign men who spoke a foreign tongue,

I learned new songs in their tongue, but 'twas songs of sorrow I sung.

If slavery was not bad enough, they added to my shame.

They took my identity by stripping me of my name.

---

[1]Here, I am addressing how at one point in time, it seemed as if Europe had a race to obtain slaves. The Portuguese were the first to reach Africa, looking for slaves in the 1450s; then other European nations followed.

[2]Small reference to one of Langston Hughes's first and most famous poem, "The Negro Speaks of Rivers," in which he expresses the importance of rivers to Blacks, be it rivers in America or back in Africa.

The slavers wanted me to think no more of where I came

Because in their minds it would make me more tame.

At that time, I could still remember who I was; it made me proud.

Just as Kunta Kinte[3] rebelled, I too shouted my true name out loud!

They whipped my back generously with the lash,

And they still talked down to me as if I were trash.

Now my history they have shrouded in mystery;

The fact that we were kings was almost a myth to me.

I asked: How could this be?

Was there a time when the African was free?

Convenient that all of my history books omit

A time that Africa had Black kings who ruled it.

It's a white man's fairy tale, so I looked for the Black man's truth;

I sifted through pages and investigated as if I were a sleuth.

How come we do not learn of a single African king,

But everyone knows of Leif Erikson, the Viking?

---

[3]Kunta Kinte was the ancestor of Alex Haley, the author of *Roots*. It is believed that Kinte was of the Mandinka tribe in Gambia, Africa. In the book and the show, Kinte refuses to go by his slave name and defies his masters by stating his true African name when asked to respond with "Toby," his slave name.

I was born by the river but not in a little tent or a hut,[4]

For I was a Black prince; you could tell by my strut.

You housed empires like that of Mansa Musa I of Mali.[5]

How many know he was the richest king in all of history?

Before the colonizers came you were a fruitful womb,

But now your name is synonymous with "desolate tomb."

The world wants to tarnish your reputation

As if they were not the cause of your situation.[6]

---

[4]Small reference to Sam Cooke's song "A Change Is Gonna Come," specifically the opening line that says, "I was born by the river, in a little tent." Here, I am stating that our African roots may not have been so humble as we think because there were kingdoms and empires that we do not learn about.

[5]Mansa Musa (1280-1337) was a West African king and ruler of the Mali Empire. He is considered the richest ruler in history, estimated to have had a net worth of 400 billion dollars at today's value. He was known for having so much gold that on his travels he would just hand it out to people he saw.

[6]Many people today, especially in the West, look down on Africa as a continent of primitive people plagued with poverty, disease, and famine. Some of them even get angry that our countries in the West send aid. What they do not understand or acknowledge is that their ancestors are the cause of Africa's situation today. Slavery removed millions of Blacks with skills from the continent, and the colonization that followed did not help. The European nations that colonized Africa carved up the country however they wanted, regardless of tribal boundaries. The colonizers did horrible things to the natives, such as King Leopold mutilating Blacks in the mines. Those are just some things that the West has done. The Europeans built off of an already existing slave trade that began in the 600s when the Arabs invaded Africa. Over nine million Africans were enslaved in Arab slave trade alone.

Black was all I knew before the land of the American,

So when the colonizers came, I asked: Is this a skinless man?[7]

Now, I see more than just Black and white; I see yellow, brown, and even red!

But, alas, their history here, too, is one of dread.

I live in a harmony of cultures, but I cannot find my voice,

And it is all because I was not brought here by choice.

Mother, I want to come home, but where do I start?

Am I from the coast or the center, closer to your heart?[8]

I have as of now no sense of belonging;

To find my family, I will be longing;

Until my true name I can discover,

I will be the orphan who does not know his mother.

---

[7] A character in *Beloved* by Toni Morrison would refer to white people as this; she had only been around Blacks.
[8] Black people know they are from Africa, but don't know from where exactly on the continent.

BLESSED ASSURANCE

Father, I call into question this blessed assurance

And the need to invest in this heavenly insurance.

They say: Follow the Good Book, and you'll have a blessed life.

My leaders all did, but they still had strife.

Saying goes: He who lives by the sword dies by the sword.

Well, they still got cut down, despite serving the Lord.

Nat Turner revolted and in You put all of his hope.

His end came on the gallows, his neck snapped by a rope.

Medgar Evers thought in You he would not lack;

His end came on his driveway, shot in the back.

Dr. King spoke and lived by the words Jesus said;

His end came on a balcony with a bullet to the head.

What about those four little girls blown up in Birmingham?[9]

Or those nine people shot while worshiping the Lamb?[10]

Both incidents happened within the walls of a church,

And now, Father, for an answer I search.

Where art Thou, O Shepherd? Look after Your sheep!

---

[9]Bombing of a predominantly Black Birmingham church; it killed four little girls on September 15, 1963.
[10]Charleston Church massacre in 2015 carried out by Dylann Roof. He killed nine Black people at a historical Black church.

Now, Thy servants lie in eternal sleep.

Where was their hedge of protection when they needed it most?

Where was the omnipresent Holy Ghost?

I do not want to think that their work was in vain,

But now I wonder if it was worth all the pain.

Love did not conquer hate,

Nor did it help their fate.

Convince me that this insurance is one I should buy,

While I look at the faces of their children cry.

Now, God, may I ask are You real?

Was my devotion just an emotion I feel?

Father, how could You leave us alone in our plight,

And let our oppressors in our pain take delight?

Was it not enough, all of our prayers and tears?

I'm not talking three days; this was 400 years!

Lo and behold, to my dismay,

Our struggles continue to this day.

I say this now; I don't want confrontation.

These questions are sincere; I need affirmation.

Now, I ponder if this religion is worth it;

I contemplate if, perhaps, I should forfeit.

Father, if You're real, please give me some of your grace;

I'm just trying to understand the suffering of my race.

TO CERTAIN "CHRISTIANS"

You infuriate me with that smile,

That blissful smile.

And with your talk of love for one another.

And your signs, insincere,

Meaningless. "Come as you are."

Within the walls

Are condescension and rejection

And closed-off minds

And ignorant sheep praying

Your recitation of empty words.

WHO BUT MY BROTHERS?

I stood outside upon my release

As these men approached, called the Police.

He was riding

Down the hood, glaring at me!

I got flashbacks in my head of what happened down the block,

Of a young brother shot dead because of some cop with a GLOCK,

Or another who was arrested

On some false charges.

I said, O Christian Brothers, if you are kind,

Save me from that cop who wants to beat my behind!

Don't let me be another news story!

But the Brothers did not assist.

The Police caught me, and I dared not resist.

And their guns they drew

Shooting at me!

Now, I do not comprehend

Why Christian Brothers don't stand up for men

Peacefully fighting injustice.

Being Black and meek,

I've been told to turn the other cheek.

So who but my Brothers

Will have my back?

Y'all are whack.

THE CROSS I BEAR

I've said things that make my colleagues stare

When I praise Malcolm it makes them glare

They don't understand my Black skin makes me an heir

Because my cross was one you never had to bear

I AM AT WAR

I declare I am at war.

Some will think it's Black-folk lore.

In the South, we have good manners,

And we also fly two banners,

The Civil War never came to an end;

There is a past descendants can't amend.

Across the street, foes wave battle flags in my face;

At school, enemies tried to put me in my place,

I've stared into their bright-colored eyes,

That looked back with contempt and despise.

This began in the year 2008;

So many children speaking words of hate,

All because our new president was Black.

And as for compassion there was a lack;

The children of rebels used words of men.

Fathers taught them "the South will rise again."

A rebel rode down the road in full Klan attire;

I thought this is the day our nation will expire.

This was when Trump won the election;

My Facebook "friends'" posts caused reflection.

Finding my enemies is not a difficult search;

I can find them among "brethren" in the walls of church.

People have asked: You're at war? At war with who?

If you must ask, perhaps I'm at war with you.

MY BLACK LIFE MATTERS

My life matters;

I hope you agree.

My life matters;

I want to be free.

My life matters;

My color isn't a choice.

My life matters;

You must hear my voice.

My life matters;

Chant 'til it don't make sense.

My life matters;

Why do you take offense?

Black lives matter;

Black lives matter

GOTTA ASK

Pardon, may I interject?

Sign says: Serve and Protect.

Gotta ask:

Whom do you serve

When you throw me on the curb?

Gotta ask:

I thought street graffiti was illegal,

Yet Black blood stains streets. Did you need to be lethal?

Gotta ask:

Did you cry when Christ hung on a tree?

What about when they did it to me?

REAL AMERICAN HORROR STORY

We don't need monsters of fiction,

We have real ones that cause our affliction.

THE DEVIL YOU KNOW

Only devils I ever known were white,

Only devils I ever known wore white.

DEATH PARADE

Crowds of whites make me nervous.

Black body surrounded by white faces,

Hands tearing flesh like unholy communion,

Blood spills like wine from a bottle,

Hanging body from a tree,

For all the world to see.

Jesus died like this for you and me,

So we wouldn't have to, too, supposedly.

When the Israelites were enslaved,

God was silent for 400 years 'til they were saved.

When their kingdoms fell to foreign hands,

They were spread across strange lands,

God was silent for 400 years between the two Testaments,

When Jesus finally came to stir sentiments.

He did it for us, they say every Sunday;

They tell us he died because we stray.

The Lamb's Blood is supposed to cover all,

But what if the blessing only extends to y'all?

You whites with blue eyes that glare,

With a rage that strips our women bare,

Take what they want from us without a care,

Never for Negroes a single thought to spare

Us from such a violent end.

They're bold; they don't pretend

For a second to be our species kin;

They don't see killing us as a sin.

Let me tell you more about lynchin'.

Did you know they'd use our skin?

Understand the totality of racist disease

When you learn about Nat Turner's grease.[11]

Lynching is white rage,

Take a nigger out the cage,

Sentenced to death without fair trial.

There's nothing fair, and life is vile;

Convicted of a crime you didn't commit,

Sometimes no crime even that they admit.

There's no jury of your peers, so no one can acquit.

They'd pull us out the jail and spit,

---

[11]Nat Turner led a slave rebellion in 1831. He was captured months later and hung. Afterwards, his corpse was skinned, turned into souvenirs (like purses and pieces of furniture) and made into grease. Some of these products were passed down through generations by those white families.

First offense with some pretext.

Faint of heart, don't read what's next.

The mob appears like a fair is in town,

When they string you up, they won't cut you down,

Human piñata for them crackers.

I call 'em crackers 'cause crackers crack.

They crack your skull.

They crack your ribs.

They crack your legs.

They lay hands upon their prey,

While you stir and start to pray,

"The end is near, this much is true.

Please, God, let it soon be through!"

But the show ain't over 'til they say it's done.

Crackers bring their kids because it's fun.

It's fun to them to stab you in the gut,

Their eyes wide open and yours shut.

Oh, and don't forget a souvenir.

They cut off your nose.

They cut off your fingers.

They cut off your ears.

They'll take whatever they want with ease.

They'll stab wherever they please.

Mementos at the cost of your strife,

They have what they want; now, they'll take your life.

Black body beaten red and blue,

America's true colors showing through.

You being hoisted up by the rope,

Pain so unbearable you can't cope,

Your life is over; there's no hope.

The neck gives out, and the body slopes.

You think death means the parade is over?

You're dead wrong; it's time for the bonfire.

White kids sit on their fathers' shoulders,

Lipless smiles gathered to admire

Lifeless corpse set ablaze with gasoline.

Blood left a stain that even Jesus can't clean.

They look you dead in the face,

What they say is what they mean;

They hate the entire Black race;

No further evidence is needed for my case.

It's been 400 years, God; pick up the pace.

Nobody is coming; keep your head out the white clouds.

Jesus ain't up there, coming down to stop white crowds.

Perhaps God's salvation has an exception;

Even in God's Law whites have exemption.

THIS TABLE

You offering me a seat

At this table?

You think it an act of kindness.

You think it an act of generosity.

How dare you insult me

By offering me a seat at this table.

Do you know anything about this table?

Know anything about its craftsmanship?

My father's father's father's father

Built this here table.

'Twas his arms that swung

And knocked down the tree.

'Twas his hands that crafted

The raw wood and made for you

A table with the finest detail.

It was he who put in the work to build it.

It was his sweat that fell from his brow,

His blood that was spilled in the work.

Do you understand me now?

That's my blood.

Why should I have to earn a seat

At the table my blood built?

Why should I be okay with scraps,

A seat,

When this is my table?

You the ones that should be asking me

For a seat.

I won't ask for a seat at the table;

I'm claiming this table.

The work of my blood incarnate,

My legacy is this table.

I'm taking what's mine.

"WHAT'S THE PROBLEM?"

So what seems to be the problem?

I can put it in a song, but you won't listen to it.

I can write it in an essay, but you won't read it.

I can write it in a poem, but you won't bother to understand it.

I can give you the books and articles, but you'll say that's in the past or it's biased.

So what seems to be the problem?

It's YOU.

You don't wanna admit that there's a problem.

It doesn't affect you, so why would you care?

I can try so many ways to make you understand, and you still won't get it.

Maybe someone should oppress you for 400 years

And make you fight for your rights,

But even then you're too selfish to care.

One SLIGHTEST inconvenience

And you claim your pain is greater than mine or of anyone of my kind.

You're the abuser,

Yet you wanna play the victim.

Now, how the fuck does that work?

I AM

You will say I blaspheme. But you blasphemed me.

You reject my art. You ignore the art of my people.

You white it out. You focus on what you made.

What you made is a mess.

You tore the fabric of Mother Africa's beautiful tapestry and ripped it to shreds across the ocean.

God creates; you destroy. Are you created in God's image?

I am of the first man. I was here first; I am the Alpha.

My people long endure. We will be the Omega.

Our spirit is immortal. God created the universe out of chaos.

We were created out of the chaos. He created everything out of nothing,

We created something out of the nothing. You told us for generations we were lesser.

You were wrong. Not lesser than you, lesser than God.

But still I am.

I am god.

I AM II

I am the much hated,

The mixed but melanited,

Message long awaited

Of a man ill-fated.

I wasn't born; I was created.

I was meditated,

Mind-state elevated.

Words I say calculated,

Me and myself were segregated.

Wickedness and weakness now consolidated,

I free those mentally incarcerated.

My ancestors' wills consecrated,

Those who listen will be educated.

I am the X-Communicated.

I AM III

When life is at its darkest, I create.

And you doubt I am?

When life is chaotic, I create order.

And you still doubt I am?

I am of the first man, and I will be the last.

That makes me Alpha and Omega.

There are three in Me.

I am god.

BLACK BEFORE

I am Black before anything.

Before I am a son,

I am a Black Son.

Before I am a man,

I am a Black man.

Before I am American,

I am a Black American.

Before I am a Colombian,

I am a Black Colombian.

I can't afford to forget because you won't let me forget.

STILL WE RISE

So many hands held us down during slavery.

They took away our original names and everything else,

Stripped it away with the lash.

Held us back physically and didn't let us read or write,

So when we were free, what could we possibly see?

How would we know

Anything about how the world is?

But we learned, and we learned quick,

And we caught up *snap* like that!

We caught up and advanced within a few years, and even in the same generation,

Not to mention the laters.

They've done all they can to hold us back,

But

Still We Rise.

THE LORD'S SIDE

I was leaning on the Lord's side,

And He moved,

But not closer

To me.

The Lord moved away.

He disappeared,

And to this day, I'm still not free.

CURSED LAND

I live on cursed land.

Cursed with the blood of Natives,

Spilled for the greed of wanting more and more.

Cursed with the blood of the Mexican people

Who died in unjust wars so the white man could have his land.

Cursed with the blood of my ancestors

Who bled picking cotton. Bled getting beat.

Bled for freedom. Bled even after we were "free."

Still bleeding to this day.

That's how I know this land is still cursed.

THE SYSTEM

You can't fight the programming

And still be in the program.

You hate the white man

But you lay with him.

You hate the white man,

But you lay with his daughters.

One way or another, whitey

Is still in you.

WHERE ARE YOUR PAPERS?

Where are your papers

Saying that you're free?

Where are your papers

Saying you belong in the

Land of the Free?

Where are your papers?

Where are your papers?

Where are your papers?

¿Donde están tus papeles?

ABOLITION

They didn't teach us about our ancestors

On Purpose.

I'm not just talking about those in Africa.

I'm talking about the ones here,

The ones that rebelled,

The ones that led the Underground,

The ones that were enslaved but not slaves.

They don't want us to know all we endured

And certainly not how we overcame.

Because learning about their tactics

From Before

Has shed light on what tactics to use now.

Use what they had and more

Media and social media.

Sway the heart,

Sway the mind.

We need to be organized like before.

Talk in Codes, Hideouts, Ally Tests.

Some of us need be ghosts, myths,

Go underground. and lead the Underground.

You can be aboveground in the Underground.

Yes, some faces will need to be seen,

But most should work behind the scenes.

FATHERHOOD USA

My father's father's father's father's mother
Was raped by a white man,
And so our bloodline came to be.
So many bloodlines started that way,
white men taking Black women
And bearing a seed in a Garden
That wasn't theirs,
But they thought they had a right to it,
To the fruit of the women.
They had children that were simply
Free labor, more property,
Not children, no blood right in the bloodline.
Abandoned children within eyesight,
Abandoned in the fields.
As far as the rightful fruit borne in gardens,
Made in love,
Those fathers were sent and sold away.
Real fathers who claimed their seed,
Forced away, unable to stay.
Yet you call us "absent fathers."

How many good, real fathers taken away?

How many absent fathers without a choice?

Not just back in the day.

I mean, to this day,

Tell me how much has really changed?

Black fathers taken away in chains,

And yet you call us "absent fathers."

DECEPTION

Elections just feel like "who gonna hold me down next"

Don't none of these candidates ever hold it down.

LIFE IN THE BIG CITY

Same city. Different sides

Same city. Different lives.

MASTERMIND

My brother pulled the trigger,

But a white man pulled the strings.

PROGRESS

Is this progression a good thing?

Have we progressed well?

I look around this room and wonder

What's going to be obsolete in here

In 10 years,

In 25 years,

In 50 years,

In 100 years?

If we make it that long,

What will last?

Will we be here to see it?

Or will we not last much longer?

I ponder as earth spins towards impending doom.

LISTEN TO ME SCREAM

How many times do I have to say it?

How many times do I have to scream it?

How many different ways do I have to try?

What's it going to take?

We've tried everything you can think of.

It's in literature, speeches, songs, dances, political movements, etc.

Why won't you listen?

Don't you care to help as you say you do?

You said you would do anything,

But you aren't doing anything.

They cripple us, yet you ask us to carry you.

But you're the ally.

You're supposed to be helping us.

So why does it seem as if we're always helping you?

We help you learn.

We put it in songs so you'll listen.

We write it in books so you'll read it.

We say it in every way possible.

But you refuse those things;

You want us to hold your hand.

We're in a fight for our lives,

We don't have time to stop

And teach you.

Our children can't afford to wait another day,

Because tomorrow it could be them on the news.

We are cursed on this earth.

Each generation is tasked with pushing ahead;

We build off our ancestors

For our collective future as a people.

Across the diaspora, our color connects us.

We cannot afford to stop for you

When you get mad at being confronted with your own ignorance,

When you don't want to do the work you claimed you wanted to do,

When you don't learn, despite claiming you want to be taught.

No, what you want is to be spoon-fed.

Nobody brings babies to a protest.

You can't bring adult babies to the Revolution.

You aren't helping if you're like this.

You're a hindrance to the movement

When you make us cease movement.

Be honest with yourself first

And simply admit you're not up to the task.

I'd rather know you won't be reliable

Than to rely on you and have you flip.

If you can't stand with us,

Then get out of the way.

THE TREE OF MIGHT

Look at how they cut our roots.

They transplanted us hundreds of years ago across an ocean

And spread us across two continents.

How did we survive it all?

Look at the fruits of our labor,

The culture we created, the land we built.

See how far our branches extend.

We have new roots now and they're firmly wound into the ground.

We overcame, we survived, and perhaps someday we will truly thrive.

This is the tree of might, and we're outta sight.

BLACK SOLES

Black feet that touched upon the earth

Heaven sent to be a seed

That sprouted the human family tree,

Black feet that walked across the earth.

THE EXILED CHILD II

Dear Mother,

Long ago, I asked you for my true name.

I told you what they had done to me since they separated us.

I see now that you have forgotten my name too.

I no longer have a home to come back to anymore.

My brothers and sisters who stayed with you do not want me and the Stolen to return.

They speak down to us as if we had a choice in leaving.

They speak down as if we had a choice on how we survived here.

I told you about how our captors took away everything.

Our native tongue, much of our culture, our family, our names.

I tell you now that we made our own culture here.

A culture forged in struggle, but ours nonetheless.

We gave ourselves names,

Names unique to us that our captors still can't understand.

We created a vocabulary that the rest of the world has tried to learn

After they fought so hard to take away our original language.

We were never given the seat at the table, so we built our own.

We built this house, Momma.

We built and rebuilt it over and over again.

Things aren't perfect here,

But we've made a way to survive on our own.

I don't know about my ancestors from the Motherland,

But I know about my ancestors here. In the Fatherland.

I know about our struggles and our pain.

I've heard about yours and what they did to you after we were stolen.

It feels as if the world is against us.

Our oppressors here, there, everywhere.

Their influence in the world wherever you go.

The distance of time and space has become too great for us now, Momma.

I've accepted that I can never come home,

For if I do, nobody will recognize me.

So I'll stay here, in the house I built.

I'll stay and survive here.

I'll have to accept that my biological mother would not have me,

But I still had one who loved me.

Maybe someday we will all be free.

I gave myself a name, and no one can take that from me.

Sincerely,

The Exiled Child

GRAY AREA

I live in a Black-and-white world,

And every now and then, I see shades of gray.

The fact is still the same; it's a dark world.

GREAT-GREAT-GREAT-GRANDMOMMA TRAUMA

Didn't take long for me to ponder that I don't like Black & white together.

Romantically, specifically, is what I mean. Especially Black Women with white men.

Call me what you will, and say what you want, but I have my reasons. Just hear me out.

Makes me think of my great-great-great-grandmomma and the way she would have had to get pregnant to have "Yellow Henry." You catch my drift?

I wonder how many others' great-great-grandmommas went through the same thing. And now that dark evil and rot are in our DNA.

Not by choice, that was never a choice. Just another thing taken from our ancestors. And another thing unwantedly given.

I think about how so many things are the same now as they were before, and I wonder if this is one more

Similarity that we share somehow, even if we're convinced that it's a choice.

Is it a choice? On our part?

I don't know. But the thought lingers. In neither case does the white truly appreciate and understand the Woman.

He is incapable and unable.

THE OWL IN THE OLD OAK TREE (IMITATION OF MEDITATION XVII)

By chance when I pass the old oak tree, what name will the owl give me this time? I take my late-night walk past the old oak tree several nights a week on my way back home from work, and he is always there, without fail, saying, "Who, who, who, who, who is next? Who do you seek?" That is what I hear that no one else seems to. Strange thing is, the only tree he perches in is this old hanging tree where people of my color were lynched. The United States of America is many separate pieces creating one big puzzle. Each state is unique with its laws and geography. How did we get to where we are today? This is the land that our ancestors forged; all of us are immigrants here, whether by force or by will. The British, the Italians, the Irish, and even some French Creoles, I know all had ancestors who crossed the Atlantic in search of a new beginning. My ancestors were thrown onto their boats in chains and shipped across the ocean like human parcels. However we got here, willingly or not, we created this country. All of us made America with the sweat of our brow and the blood we shed for its freedom. Despite our shared history, our common struggle, there are those who would keep us separate simply for being shades darker than the other.

I look upon this old oak tree, and I think about the tree of life, the one Reverend Poe describes on Sundays in the book of Revelation. God is the gardener, and He plants the seed into the earth. We are a literal family tree, with our roots going deep into the ground from the start of creation. Each generation is grafted onto this tree, causing it to branch out more and more. At the branches, we all bear fruit. Some of us bear good fruits that God desires from us, so He lets us stay where we are. However, there are other branches that bear fruit so rotten that

God has no choice but to cut them off as to prevent the whole tree from going bad.

The greatest contradiction in the world lies here in the center of my city, for beside this hanging tree is an apple tree that bears the sweetest apples I have ever tasted. I stand back far enough to observe them both. My city has its own tree of life and tree of knowledge of good and evil, like in the book of Genesis. That old oak tree that used to bear such bitter and forbidden fruit. What a strange thing, when the fruit of this tree was ripe, it would swell to the point of bursting if nobody was brave enough to pluck it from where it hung. This is the forbidden knowledge to some who would rather, as they say, "put the past behind us."

My parents think otherwise. They tell me what the old oak tree used to bear before laws were put in place to prevent fruit from growing on it ever again. There are those in the city who want to cut the tree down and do away with our tree of knowledge of good and evil. I say leave it; ignorance cannot be our bliss. Let this tree stand as a reminder of the injustice that ran rampant in our nation's shared history. Let this tree stand to remind us of the evils that men are capable of. Let this tree show everyone who walks past it what discrimination leads to.

I look up and wonder how long the owl has been here. Was he perched here when the tree used to bear the forbidden fruit? Was he here announcing another name every time that the juice poured out of the fruit and onto the leaves? The tree should stay to be a testament to what we overcame. The Owl needs a place to be so that he can tell me our history.

THE DEATH NOTE

It was finally my turn,

I feared this day would come.

Pulled over on some bullshit,

My car forever left in park,

Sudden flash and now it's all dark.

I can see my body,

You can see me too,

They took a video,

It went viral.

Look Mom, I'm on the news,

How many views?

Millions come to see me,

Now what am I?

What am I to you?

Another dead nigga,

Another chant in the street,

Another face on a shirt,

Another name added to the list,

Another brother dead without a cause,

Another ancestor to hear your despair,

Another one gone too soon.

You'll march and you'll chant in my name,

I'll watch you from above and beyond,

No justice, no peace.

Know justice, know peace.

I see your posters,

I see you posers,

I see you posting,

I join my Ancestors.

I'm among the damned,

No damn justice,

I'm among the thousands,

I'm among the millions,

Of dead Blacks who died

With no justice.

My trial most unfair,

All I could do was stare.

My brother hugged my killer,

And granted them forgiveness.

My anger burns like the fire you set,

Thank you for the flames,

I gladly accept your offering of pain,

Your offering of anger.

I am not my brother,

I am my Ancestors,

I am your Ancestor.

Don't listen to my brother,

He didn't know me,

He doesn't speak for me,

They don't know Us.

What we want isn't justice,

They're a million deaths too late,

They're 700 years too late.

We want flames,

Burn it all down,

Their monuments are obscene,

I'll join you in the flames.

When you scream I scream too!

How many of us will it take?

How many deaths before it comes?

The prophetic revolution,

The pathetic institutions,

That tried to cover it up,

You'll never shut us up,

Even if you can't hear it,

I hope you fear it.

How much more blood must be spilled?

What's it going to take?

They've killed so many of us,

We've had enough.

Don't listen to your false prophets,

We didn't move on,

I can say this without a doubt,

As sure as I'm Black,

I'm here and I'm mad,

Still here and I'll linger.

The flames have died down,

They've washed it all away,

The crowd is gone.

Some of you already forgotten my name,

I'm on the long list that keeps growing,

I know I won't be the last,

I can't blame you for forgetting,

Too many names to remember,

It's hard to keep up,

For those that remember,

Thank you,

I'll see you at the next one.

THE ORCA: LIFE IN BLACK & WHITE

I swam in the vast ocean,

I was the king of the seas,

Despite what you think,

Greater than the Great whites,

They swim deeper when they see me.

You captured me and put me in a pool,

Trained me to do tricks like a fool,

I could swim the seven seas,

My life could go in any direction,

Now all I can do is swim in circles,

Jump through circles,

I was free to see the world,

Now I'm trapped in Sea World,

Life is so mundane,

Every day is the same,

I'm going insane,

Just going in circles,

Doing your little tricks,

Was it worth it?

Was the price you paid to get in,

Was the brief time you spent here,

Not even a full day just mere hours,

Worth my life in torment?

My life in bondage,

For your entertainment,

The belly colored people,

With eyes like the ocean,

The people who speak of freedom,

Love to put creatures they deem strange,

In any and every cage,

They do it to the top colored people,

The Black people.

I'll never leave this cage,

And neither will you,

So when they asked why I drowned you,

I knew this to be true,

I got my revenge and I got my life back,

I got my revenge and they killed me,

They won't release me back into the wild,

They killed me for doing what's in my name,

They killed me and they couldn't tame.

The instinct in me,

Not the desire to kill,

But the desire to be free,

I'll never leave this prison alive,

But your death has allowed my escape,

My escape from this world,

Because even in the ocean I'm not safe,

I'm dead and now I'm free.

WONDER WOMAN

Imagine you met Wonder Woman:

She's fought off muggers,

She fought off notorious narcos,

Survived explosions,

Survived terrorist attacks,

So many feats of bravery,

So many feats of Valor.

She's the strongest woman you know,

She's also the nicest woman you know.

Now imagine the day comes when a Lion attacks you:

An old toothless Lion,

Toothless but not harmless to you,

For you are just a babe with no power,

Imagine Wonder Woman sees the Lion attack,

And she just sits back and watches.

Imagine you cry out for her help,

And she just sits back and watches.

Imagine you ask her why she won't use her power,

And she just sits back and watches.

You get mauled for the Lion has strength,

And is a greater size than you,

But Wonder Woman, she has the strength to stop it,

And she does nothing.

Actually she does do something,

When you've had enough and try to fight back,

Wonder Woman steps in,

And you think "finally she's come to help me,

Perhaps together we can ward off the Lion!

Certainly we can, it's Wonder Woman!"

But instead, she steps in on behalf of the Lion,

She tells you that not only is she not going to defend you,

She doesn't want you to defend yourself,

"Let yourself be mauled,

It would be dishonorable for you to defend yourself,

Don't let it affect you."

Don't let it affect you she says,

While you stand there bleeding,

While you're crying and pleading,

Don't let it affect you while you stare at the cuts,

The kinds of cuts that scar,

The kinds of wounds that never quite heal right,

The kinds of injuries that could kill.

You realize Wonder Woman is not the hero you thought she was,

And when you do finally resist the Lion,

Wonder Woman steps in on his behalf again,

Her instinct is not to protect you,

You manage to carry yourself away,

And take one last look back at the woman you thought was

Wonder Woman,

The scars are the reminder you were wrong.

UNSPOKEN THEY

Everywhere you turn your head,

They're kneeling on our necks.

The presently invisible Them,

Those who hold the power.

Did we ever have it?

When did they take it?

Now they have it all.

LICENSE TO KILL

Wear the blue,

Protect the blue,

Wear the gray,

Get out the way,

They comin through,

Not to protect you,

Protect the State.

State interest,

No concern to you,

State interstate,

State trooper,

No concern for you.

Stopped you cold,

You lyin cold.

Black and blue,

And Red all over

The news.

Yesterday's paper,

Twenty-four hour news,

Gave ya momma the blues.

License to drive in any state,

Red lights whoop whoop

Now you gettin' whooped.

One wrong turn sealed your fate,

Boys in blue got License too,

Boys dressed in blue,

And sometimes gray too,

Got the License to kill you.

SISTER SLUG

Slug I mistook for a leach,

Get up on Sunday and preach.

Tell 'em your lies!

Tell 'em your truth!

It's me you despise,

Hated since youth.

Thou shalt not gossip,

Tea too good, you had to sip.

Drink my cup of wrath,

Lake of fire is your bath.

The Great I Am you insult,

Your church is a cult.

Sing and dance and praise,

Memorize every phrase.

Jumpin' and havin' a fit,

Laid out on the floor.

Look down from your pulpit,

Look down at the poor.

Walking down Fifth Avenue,

But you didn't spread Good News.

Too busy lookin' for new shoes,

Recite verses like your cues.

It's all an act, you put on a show,

One day you'll reap what you sow.

The Bible really a book you read?

You know you a bad seed?

Ignored their cries and woes,

Almost stepped on my toes.

Yous a pimp and you got hoes,

Yes men and shiny clothes.

Yes men and "Yes Lawd!"

This is blasphemy, my God!

Why won't anyone stop the program?

Everybody just waving their program.

No ma'am, this ain't right,

Truth would give these folks fright.

Money for the church lines your pockets,

Pastor used it to buy you new lockets.

Thousands of souls being lead astray,

You run a good con, how'd you get this way?

How you take the Good News

And make the blues?

Run you blind sheep!

It's a wolf wearing white!

Lie so easy, what a creep.

This bark is worse than a bite.

False Prophet only cares for profits,

Shop til you drop, got the money to cop it.

What a waste of a good voice,

You a sinner-saint by choice.

Want some gossip to share?

Read this to 'em, I dare.

Your sin is sloth and slug,

This the tea, bring your mug.

FRO GOT TO GO

Black skin with a curly crown,

It made me sad, I had to frown,

When yo momma said to cut it down.

Got to look good for the white folk!

Lies I despise, what a sick joke.

I'm upset, not trynna sound woke.

Cut off your crown for the job,

So the crackers won't call you a slob,

Some dude in a tie, probably a snob.

Shaved or straight, the vibe is killed,

You grew it so long, took years to build,

Just to hear, "the position has been filled."

LOSING RECIPES

There once was a house of many rooms,

But now they're alone, like empty tombs.

Remember the chicken that grandma fried?

Nobody's cooked it since the day she died,

Nobody could even if they tried,

Yet another reason I cried.

TRADING PLACES

I spoke to my brother the other day,

He said he wanted to leave the USA.

He went to Congo, back to the Motherland,

And he met our cousin who was missing a hand,

He was shook because nobody had told

Him about the terror of King Leopold,

Let's just say Belgian goods came at a price,

Nothing the Europeans did in Africa was nice.

A Nigerian cousin was tired of Buhari,

She moved to the UK but she was soon sorry

That she had left home and her throne,

Now she faced slurs and hate always thrown

At her just because of her dark skin,

Britain was not a place she could win.

Mi primo del Caribe

Was tired of Uribe

So he came to visit the States,

He's got no clue of what awaits.

He thought this was a safe place to roam,

But the xenophobes told him to go home.

I warned my long lost uncle not to come here,

He laughed and said "I have nothing to fear!

Yes I'm Black, but I'm not Black like you."

I said "oh my poor uncle you haven't a clue."

When the boys in blue killed his son, he was blue,

He said "I can't believe this happened to me too!"

Trade places across the Diaspora as much as you want,

The demons that plagued our ancestors remain to haunt,

Running away can only get you so far,

Travel by air, by train, or by car,

I speak plainly so that there's no confusion,

Trading places is a temporary solution.

You see we're a family of all shades and places,

I love you all and I love your smiling faces,

But there's a truth that none of us can escape,

You're Black in this world no matter the landscape,

There's nowhere to run from our plight,

We have no choice but to fight.

ESTÁ BERRACO

Soy Negro aquí, soy Negro allá,

Primo te digo, no venga pa'ca.

Aquí en los Estados,

Tambien eramos esclavos.

No persiga el sueño americano,

No es verdad, sería en vano.

Yo se que donde estás la cosa está dura,

Odiar el Negro aquí es parte de la cultura.

ACTS OF SERVICE

They promised I'd be free,

So I joined their army.

I fought in their "Revolution,"

I thought it was our solution.

The war was won but thanks to greed,

Not a single Negro was actually freed.

A new promise was made in 1863,

So I signed up for the Union army.

I marched down to the sea with Sherman,

This time we'll be free; I was certain.

I gave it my all, I fought the good fight,

Lincoln said we'd finally have the right.

We was promised 40 acres and a mule,

That was a lie and I felt like a tool.

Used like a slave but under a new master,

No punishment for the rebel bastards.

Sharecropping kept me on the plantation,

This was my reward, just more damnation.

In 1917 I joined the army,

We had a goal from Booker T.

If we fight hard overseas,

Then our oppression would cease.

We fought hard, we fought like hell,

But Black veterans still weren't treated well.

Coming back to America wasn't just a bummer,

Our reward for our service? It was called the Red Summer.

I prayed for our suffering to come to pass,

They burned towns and killed us in mass.

I joined yet again in World War 2,

I'd heard about Pearl Harbor on the news.

Our campaign was for double victory,

This time was our time, it had to be.

Nazi prisoners were treated better than us,

We Blacks still had to ride at the back of the bus.

When Uncle Sam started the Vietnam War,

I thought, "What for? What's war good for?"

Uncle Sam got mad that I raised my voice,

"This is a draft, you don't have a choice!"

I fought in the war and I'm glad that we lost,

All this death, it wasn't worth the cost.

Every time I signed up I felt like a fool,

I see kids sign up now, thinking they cool.

I'll tell you a secret you won't learn in school,

The truth of this nation, a truth rather cruel.

They're all the same, don't make a mistake,

They promise freedom but it's all fake.

Washington and the founders called for liberty,

But most of them owned slaves, that's the bitter tea.

Lincoln didn't fight to free the slaves,

He thought we might as well live in caves.

You thought Kennedy was a remedy,

They're all tools of white supremacy.

Johnson was good, or that's what you figure,

Behind your back he'd call you a nigger.

You can fight and die for them and that is your right,

But know this, Blacks will never have rights known to whites.

It's the truth that I had to learn,

Listen or you'll be ashes in an Urn.

This freedom is not one you can earn,

Black plight was never their concern.

Look at history, can't you see?

This is American democracy.

REDBONE BLUES

Redbone boy,

Loved the blues

Since I was a babe.

Electric guitar

Electric to my senses.

(Goosebumps on my skin)

Pierced my ears,

Pierced my heart,

Pierced my soul.

Infant's body

With an old soul.

I told ya I been here

Before.

Redbone baby

That loved the blues

Writes what he knows

Deep in his soul.

Redbone writes the blues

When he's feeling blue.

Redbone but always blue.

MAROON BOY

Maroon boy stuck on this earth,

Marooned on this land,

I came here by sea,

I lived by the river,

I live by new rivers.

I live in a swamp,

I live by the sea,

I live by the water,

I escaped from the land.

I don't live with ease,

But I live how I please.

I'm nobody's slave,

I do what I want,

I work when I want.

If you don't come in peace,

You'll leave here in pieces.

We stay on our own,

On this land that we own.

DANTE'S INFERNO

Did I ever tell you about my ancestor, Dante,

Who tried to escape from Hell?

His grandfather had been taken on a trip,

Forced on a ship,

He ended up in Hell.

Dante's father was born into it,

And Dante was born into it too.

Heaven sent souls bound for Hell

On Earth.

Did I mention Cousin Virgil?

He was the one could read,

He was the one knew the words

To the song.

They followed the drinking gourd,

But,

Crossing the Ohio,

Was like crossing the Styx,

Not the River Jordan.

They made it past the River,

They barely escaped

From the South,

And made a life elsewhere.

Slavery eventually ended,

Sometime after they ascended

To the North.

But Hell is still Hell,

No matter what you call it.

They couldn't reach Paradise,

It can't be seen with a brown pair of eyes,

In America.

They hadn't escaped Hell,

They'd gone up to another circle of it.

DANTE'S PURGATORIO

We lost a lot of them,

During those trips,

Around the Sun.

We prayed to many gods,

We fought for many causes,

We had many kingdoms.

We as Black folk,

We as humanity as a whole,

We as the global society.

We blamed many evils,

We blamed many devils,

We blamed select devils.

Now I see the truth,

Now I know what I knew,

In the beginning.

The gods you made are in you,

But so are the devils and evils,

Scapegoats for your sins.

Abolish the systems,

Crumble the empires,

Humanity remains.

Still no peace on earth,

Blame another (d)evil,

For what is humanity's truth.(?)

DANTE'S PARADISO

I'm in a field,

I woke up and I'm lost,

I sit up and see

All that were lost

Have appeared to me.

I stand and run,

I run so fast I fly,

Lost souls greet me,

Not a single tear

From any eye falls.

Love, joy, and peace,

A trinity of calm,

The essence of this place,

We're in a star up in space,

We play,

We sing,

We dance,

We speak,

I found peace.

It took leaving earth,

It took leaving life,

I'm truly alive here,

Ours souls no longer bound,

Our bodies no longer holding,

Our minds no longer pondering,

Our lives mattered,

But this matters too,

This matters more,

What's the matter?

There is no matter,

There is no work,

We understand,

We are free,

This is freedom.

They tell me things,

They teach me things,

There are no limitations,

Nothing weighs me down,

No gravity can detain my soul,

I jumped so high

I kicked an apple in a tree,

If you can swim you can fly,

I swam through the sky,

I mastered every weapon,

I pondered why,

It's a place of peace,

Full of warriors,

They taught me their craft,

I learned from the poets,

Their pens were strong,

Their pens were sharp,

I saw it all,

I learned it all,

Love was always there,

Even on earth,

But I never knew it,

They told me there.

It was the ray of sun,

On a cold day.

It was a cool breeze,

In Texas humid heat.

It was the number on a clock,

A reminder: They were there.

It was a spider,

Trapping a bug in my room.

It was my intuition,

Advice that was given.

Now I heard them clear,

They're all my dear,

And I am theirs.

Dead to the world,

Not dead to memory.

Dead to the world,

But not dead to me,

My dear Dead Darlings,

I was now among them,

Days were eternity,

Time is an illusion.

But it was time,

Time to go back,

For the first time,

In what seemed years,

Tears.

I cried.

How can I go back?

Not because I died,

How does one return,

To earth,

From being in the sun?

Closest thing to heaven,

I refused to be alone,

In a world without them,

Dead Darlings,

They whispered,

They smiled,

They said,

"You'll take us with you."

Tears stopped flowing,

It was time to get going,

They smiled,

I smiled,

I was in the field,

Surrounded in love,

Embraced by arms beyond count,

When I came I was lost,

I'll never lose again.

I closed my eyes,

I felt the warm glow,

I opened my eyes,

I awoke in the sea,

Staring up at the stars,

My Dead Darlings, greeting me.

THE BALLOT

I cast my vote, the illusion of choice,

I cast my vote, I used my voice.

I cast my vote, but who do I choose?

I cast my vote, either way I lose.

I cast my vote for the lesser of two evils,

I cast my vote, I'm tired of bad deals.

I cast my vote, I hope he's a winner,

I cast my vote, nevermind he's a sinner.

I cast my vote, this deal is a scam,

I cast my vote, whole thing is a sham.

I cast my vote, it's in God's hands,

I cast my vote, they stealing our lands.

I cast my vote, this one is my race!

I cast my vote, you lied to my face.

I cast my vote, boy you a lie!

I cast my vote, we continue to die.

I cast my vote, he said I'll be free!

I cast my vote, they all lyin to me.

I cast my vote, I'm tired of liars,

I cast my vote, this is an empire.

I cast my vote, it's all an illusion.

I cast my vote, it was all a delusion.

I cast my vote, they commit crime,

I cast my vote, this my last time.

I cast my vote into the flames.

Ballot or bullet, I'm taking the reins.

Presidents and emperors are one in the same,

Masses and revolution, I'm ending your reign.

THE BULLET

My flames are a Righteous fire,

I stand against this star-spangled empire.

Of lies and broken promises I tire,

I'll stand and fight until I expire.

No more bulletins or ballots,

I want bullets, I've had it.

Haven't been free since 1619,

There's so much evil we've seen.

Don't matter who we elect,

Don't matter how we select.

It's your choice to make, to believe what's fake,

But freedom isn't granted, it's something you take.

They've taken enough,

They're calling our bluff.

So I must insist,

Raise a fist and resist!

I Am IV

I Am the voice that speaks through the fire,

I Am the flames that will never expire.

I Am the voice that spoke to Moses,

I Am that I Am, Uncle Sam owes us.

Let my people go,

You are my foe.

It's been 400 years,

You're grinding my gears.

Let my people go,

You will face woes.

I'll set Plagues upon the land,

I'm not asking, this is a demand.

Let my people go,

Our strength will grow.

From sea to shining sea,

The people will be free.

Part Two

The Dark Corner

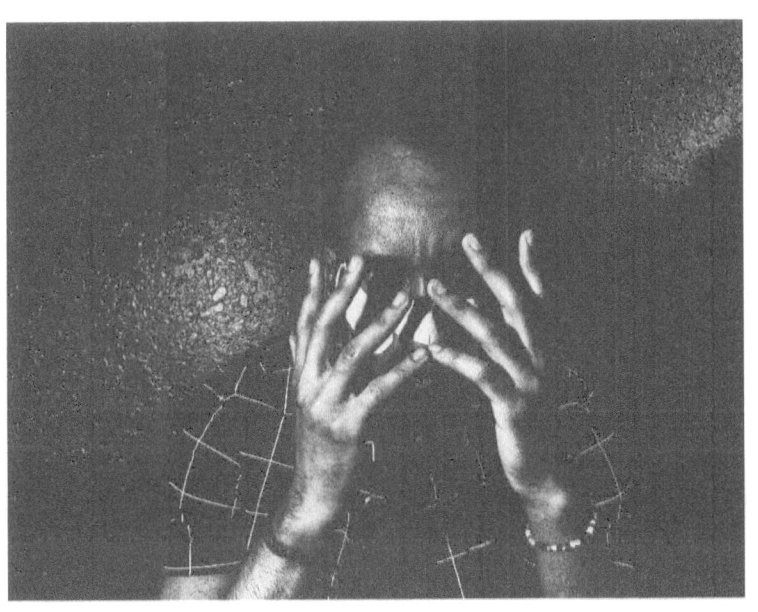

Introduction

I wrote the majority of these poems in my room at home during a depressive episode. There were many of those. Writing these poems was cathartic. I needed to write out how I felt, but talking about it wasn't enough. Simply writing in a journal wasn't enough to fully express the pits of despair that I was in.

There were songs and albums by several artists that saved my life at times or gave me words of comfort simply by letting me know I wasn't alone in what I was feeling. Some of those albums were *Because the Internet* by Childish Gambino, *Flower Boy* by Tyler, the Creator, *Pieces of a Man* by Gil Scott-Heron, and pretty much all of Kendrick Lamar's discography, but especially *DAMN*.

I started writing out my thoughts and feelings as poetry instead of doing journal entries. The poetry helped even while I was going to therapy for nine months. I made an acronym for the poems I included in this section—MTSHBAJE (pronounced "met-ish-ba-heh"), which means "Maybe This Should Have Been A Journal Entry." MTSHBAJE simply means I was going through a difficult depressive episode, and the emotions in the poems are very raw.

Some of these were never originally meant to be shared with the world. However, when I began creating this book, there was no debate as to whether or not I'd include them. I knew I wanted to add them because they are part of my poetry collection, they are works of art, and perhaps I can do for someone else what the albums and artists I spoke of earlier did for me; maybe I can give somebody else the words to express what they're feeling. Someone else who is struggling with depression can read these words and know that they're not alone because someone else feels what they're feeling. Someone else shares this pain. It makes this existential loneliness a little less lonely for a moment. Or at least helps you make sense of what you're feeling.

If you read this section and you can relate, then I want to say this to you:

I'm sorry you feel like this. It's okay to cry, to scream, to not do anything at all for a whole day because you just feel empty inside. I hope a day comes soon when you're doing something you enjoy and have a moment in which you say to yourself, "I'm glad I'm here for this." I had a lot of moments like that with my friends whom I never told.

I'm glad you're still here. Please stay.

Trigger Warning: Some of these poems may be hard to read as they deal with depression and suicide. Especially "Death Note II"

REACH

Can't get out of my bed.

Can't get out of my head.

Stuck inside the four corners of my mind.

Alone except for me, myself, and I.

Solitary confinement and no key,

Prison of my making, trapped, can't get free,

I reach out silently,

But no one can save me.

Reach out as a reaction and it's in vain.

Brain made the chain and produces the pain.

Just when you think you can win,

Depression pulls you back in.

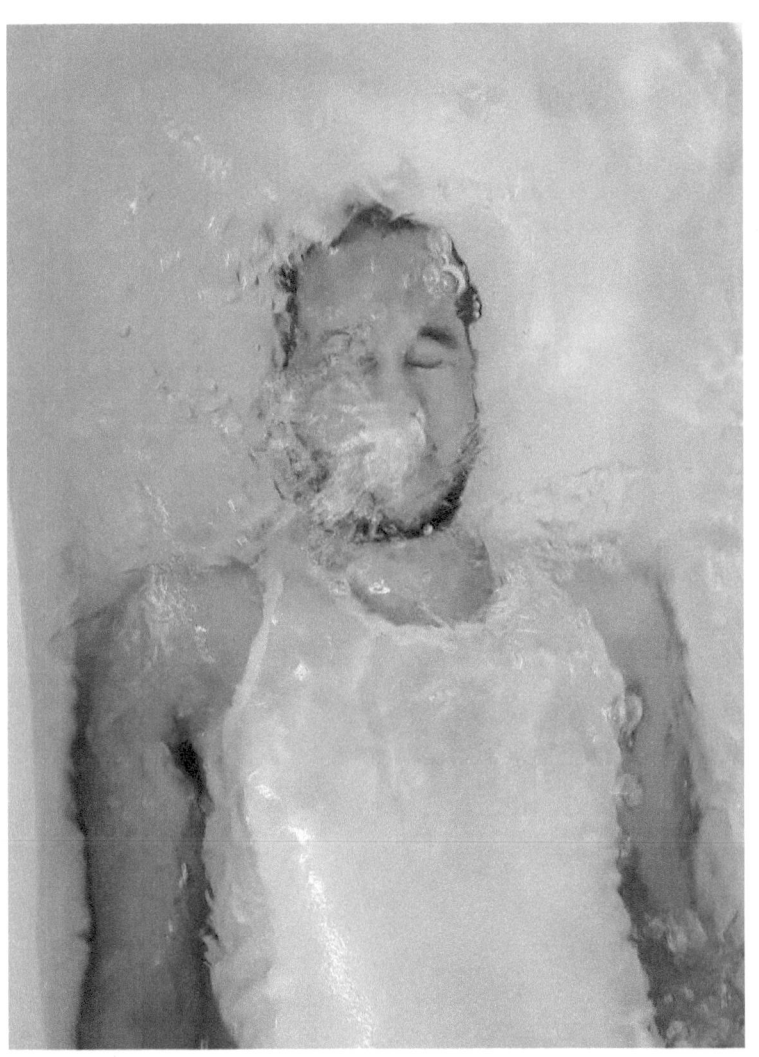

BE GONE

Everybody got somebody,

Except me, of course.

Nobody need me;

They got their somebody.

I can stay gone, and I'll miss out

On their lives,

But they won't miss mine or me.

Everybody got their somebody they tell

Everything and every secret to.

I'm nobody's somebody, so when they tell me too,

I know I'm just an extra person,

Not an essential body.

So long, everybody,

I'll be on my way.

Said I wouldn't be long,

But I don't belong,

So I'll be gone.

ISOLATION

Being away from everything and everyone,

Is as simple now as pressing "log off,"

And in one second, I'm isolated from the world.

I'm in self-imposed exile because I want

To stop looking at everyone else's lives,

And I need to focus on mine.

Isolation feels as if I'm holding my breath

Underwater.

I can see only what's around me,

Can't see or hear anybody else.

I don't know if I wanna come up for air.

Nobody comes for you.

You wonder if they know you're gone.

You wonder if you were really gone

Would they care?

I wonder what's going on in their lives.

They'd tell me if they needed me. Right?

Or maybe not,

Because the reason I'm isolated

Is because nobody needs me,

So it's okay for me to go.

IMPENDING DOOM

The earth is doomed.

No, it wasn't the Martians,

But we'll soon suffer their fate too.

It was its own inhabitants.

Earthlings killed Mother Earth

While calling each other aliens,

Instead of working together.

Instead of fixing their mess.

What do we do?

. . .

What's on TV?

I HOPE YOU SEE ME

I hope, when you look at me,

You see Me.

I hope it isn't like looking at Shaolin[12]

And realizing he's just Curtis.

I looked at God,

And realized He's just a myth.

I listened to the voice of God

And realized it was My (Higher) Self.

I looked at my father,

And I saw he was just a man

Named Elgin.

So when you look at Me,

I hope You see Me.

---

[12]Shaolin is a character from the show *The Get Down*. He is the coolest member of the group, and the others look up to him. However, he shows his true colors, and the main character, Zeke, starts to see the true Shaolin, who reveals that his real name is Curtis. This is the symbolic end to the illusion of Shaolin.

MIRROR IMAGE

When you look in the mirror,

Who looks back at you?

Do I see Me

Or some version I could be?

Who am I really?

Does anybody see Me as I am?

Do I see Myself?

Whom do you see when you look at Me?

Do you like what you see

When you look in the mirror?

CRUISE CONTROL

When I'm on autopilot

My mind keeps going,

My body keeps going,

But my body acts

On instinct and memory.

It's not conscious,

Because in my head

We're debating whether to

Keep our foot on the gas,

Step on the gas,

Get off the road,

And end the ride,

Or park the car

And work on it.

Is it worth it?

Is it fixable,

My mind?

2 YEARS

In 2 years, you'll have your second kid.

In 2 years, you'll be engaged or married,

But engaged for sure,

Maybe not in, but within, 2 years.

Within 2 years, I'll no longer be with you,

Perhaps not for the reason you think.

Maybe you wouldn't see it coming,

But I do

Because it's on my terms,

And you don't know my intentions.

You don't know that I'm expecting this to end.

I don't think I'll be there to see

(What happens in 2 years?)

Because I'll have ended our friendship,

Or at least

I know why our bonds will end.

Maybe I'm being paranoid,

But it's happened before

With other people.

It all ends because of me,

Because of how I am.

Should I enjoy the time we have left,

Or should I end it preemptively?

Either I end the friendship,

Or I end my life.

But, either way,

It ends because of me.

I end it.

I can't tell what it'll be.

Don't bet

On the 3rd option

That within 2 years

I'm still here with you.

I'll see what I said

Come true.

Don't bet on it

Because I'm usually right.

Usually.

THE STRUGGLE IS REAL

Maybe my thoughts are irrational.

I can tell when I'm not being rational,

But what if someday I can't

Talk myself out of it

Anymore.

The thoughts are irrational,

But the feelings are still real.

Maybe I'm making it up in my head,

But that doesn't make the pain less real.

My problems aren't fake

Just because I created them.

Because everything that's real

And true

To you in your head

Is real in its effects,

And it really affects me.

BFF

Friendships are temporary; music is forever.

Friends come and go;

Seldom are they forever,

But they're more likely to stay

Than a romantic partner.

Some loves feel like forever.

But I don't trust anybody fully,

Not even myself,

So I can't trust any of you to stay,

And I can't trust myself to want to

(Stay)

But the music is still here,

Even when nobody else is.

When there's nothing left,

There's no one left.

LONELY PROSE

I asked him, "Does it…get better?"

He looked at me and after only a second of silence uttered, "No."

I looked away because the truth staring me in the face was too much, but I let the gravity of it sink in. Without looking back at him, I said, "Thanks." First honest answer I'd gotten; I was truly grateful.

I had started to move when he said, "I'm not finished." I stopped and turned around. He wasn't staring in my direction anymore; he was looking at his reflection in the water. Without turning to me, he continued, "It doesn't get better; you have to make it better."

A feeling of frustration arose inside of me, and I'm sure it was written on my face, but he didn't need to look at me to know. He also knew what I was gonna ask, but he let me say my line. "How? How the hell do I do that?"

This time, he glanced at me and gently stated, "You find a way. You find what you want in this life, and you give it everything you've got. You keep living until you find that door of opportunity you're looking for, and you get your foot in there however you can. And you don't just do this for you; this is for everybody who came before you, and this is for everyone who will come after you. Just as those artists and activists inspired you by simply living their lives, you will do that for those who come after. It's what we owe them."

He adjusted to turn his body to face me now. "You see your life as a cursed existence, you don't want to be here, and I don't blame you. Depression is a bitch, and I know how powerful the mind is. I know how draining it is to fight yourself. To find yourself in an existential crisis every weekend. Life can be a gift if you live it right, though. Maybe you feel like nobody in your life cares if you're here or not, but your art can help others like you. They'll care. More people care about you right now than you know, and the more you live, the more people there will be."

He paused and went on, "You still gotta live for you. Don't you think your life matters? You wanna leave now? What if it gets better? Life goes on, and who knows what you'll miss out on. Every day is a gamble, but at least you can still bet. If you pull out of the game now, if you forfeit, you'll never know if you could have won. Maybe that's not enough either. Maybe that's not enough to fill the void, but it's something. You can still help other people somehow. Think of the artists you love so much and what they went through. Think about how they've all had their moments of doubt, moments when they wanted to end it all, but they didn't. They kept living, and now they're even more successful than they were before. The things they've created that death would not have allowed."

THE ABUSE

Mary Jane is whom I choose to spend my nights with;

Life abuses me, so I abuse drugs.

I take hits, but sometimes she's blunt and hits me back.

Mary Jane always has one hell of a time.

She brings the best and the worst out of me.

We've had our highs and lows, as any couple on Facebook would say,

But she's been there for my highs and lows,

And she knows all my woes.

This shit ain't toxic; it's what God gifted man.

Kind of fucked up that I gotta keep her a secret.

Y'all just don't get her the way I do.

She helps give me a lift and takes me high

Above the sky, outta sight from naked eye,

Can see me fly.

She helps me believe in myself,

And we party every night,

But every day I lose faith

In myself, so I come back to her by midnight.

The relationship is abusive by definition;

Maybe it's toxic, maybe, maybe, maybe,

But she's my baby,

And she's always there for me,

Until she ain't.

THE VALLEY

This path used to be ups and downs,

Good times and bad times,

But now the bad times last longer.

No more mountains I get to the peaks of and feel numb.

I've been in the valleys more.

With strength to climb up diminishing by the day,

Not even able to climb up hills as much,

I just roll back downhill.

I need help getting out of the valley,

But there's no one to reach out to.

Part of me doesn't want to have to come down

From where I am and leave the peaks or hills.

Am I selfish for wanting help?

I can't make it on my own anymore.

I split myself in three for company,

But they gave up, and they're gone.

The only voices left are the dark ones.

The light has left my mind, and all I see

Is the darkness that wants to consume me,

And I want to let it.

More often than not, I want to end it.

I don't want to fight anymore.

I'm tired of climbing.

There's no point leaving the valley

If every win still feels like a loss.

Because there's no one left to share moments with,

I think about cutting myself

Out of their lives,

Out of this life.

BRIDGES

Burned all my bridges

I'm stuck on my island

Time to build new bridges

Or maybe it's safer here

I HATE SOCIETY

Who's we?

You and me?

Is it society?

Woe is me (I say).

Woe is we (I say).

Society is a menace to me.

I wonder if my friends are tired of me,

If only we could see life in its entirety.

Is anybody real besides me?

Ain't nobody real besides me,

'Cause I hate your insincerity,

You know that it ain't fair to me.

I am the MC,

Marcus Coffee,[13]

The star of the show you came to see.

But am I who I claim to be?

Are you tired of me?

Do you conspire against me?

Who do you aspire to be?

---

[13]Marcus Coffee is an alter ego I created.

Will they look at me admirably?

These thoughts and questions come from anxiety;

My personalities come in a variety

Pack your bags and say bye already.

Depressive mind-set on "Expire When Ready."

Last meal, I'll have Mom's spaghetti.

Trigger blast feels like hot confetti.

Mood swings can't keep my thoughts steady.

Unanimous vote to cease to be,

Clouded mind with no chance of clarity,

Quality time is such a rarity,

Feels like charity.

Share with me (a moment).

Here, keep my words to remember me

When I…

Rest in peace.

THE SUNKEN PLACE

I'm trapped in my mind; I'm in the sunken place.

You can see the sign on my sulking face;

I think of the struggles of the Black race.

Game is rigged; this ain't a fair race.

Bag ain't the only thing I'm trynna chase.

My dreams help me plead the case

Against thoughts that want to erase

Me from this cursed place.

You can probably read it on my face,

But there's no one here.

The desk clear.

There's no one checking in,

So I'm checking out. Fin.

Telling you now so you know where I been.

NAIR

Neglected skin care,

I don't care.

What to wear?

A face with a blank stare,

Sometimes tempers flare,

Get met with a cold glare.

Losing my mind faster than my hair,

Call it mental Nair.

In a prison called depression,

The form of self-oppression,

Self-inflicted injuries.

My words, my actions, remember these.

THE GAME

Landed on first place where I belong.

You tried to fight, but I knew all along

My path is set. I'm chosen; this was set in stone.

Now, get the fuck up off my throne.

DREAMER

The cruelest thing my body can do to me is not allow me to sleep.

The cruelest thing in the world is to make me stay awake.

I don't enjoy life, and I don't enjoy being awake.

I'd rather sleep. When I say this, you assume laziness.

No, that's not it; everything is better in my dreams.

And if I dream lucidly, everything can be how I want it to be.

The girl you love loves you back.

There isn't so much pain in the world.

There aren't any worries or cares.

You dream and live the life you want.

That's what Martin had, a dream.

A perfect world only exists in dreams.

I don't want to wake up to reality.

The best afterlife for me is an eternal dream of my creation.

When I'm awake, I don't know what's real and what's fake.

I can't read minds or hearts, and I don't trust anyone.

It's all lies. When I'm dreaming, I know it's not real, but the feelings are real.

Is it about control? No, I think it's more about knowing.

Knowing what's felt is sincere.

Nobody can hurt me there.

Music and my mind, the ultimate escapes.

UNIDENTIFIED MALE

I put Myself to sleep.

Don't ask Me about it.

Only I know.

I did not love Myself.

I consider Myself weak.

Too weak for this world.

I could not trust Myself.

I could not bring Myself to do better.

I could not make Myself put Me first.

Others were always put ahead of Me.

So I made a decision for Me and Myself.

I did what was best for Me,

And that is why I put Myself to sleep.

Now, I am driving the boat.

I am putting Me first, before anyone else.

I am not Myself.

I am a better version of Me.

THE METHOD (OF SADNESS)

One bullet

In the chamber

That holds six.

One slice

To the wrist,

I have two.

One jump

From the bridge,

Houston has many.

One crash

Into the rails,

Highways are aplenty.

THE DEATH NOTE II

What if I die by my own hands?

What if I die by my heart stopping?

What if I die right now?

What if you could know my final thoughts?

There wouldn't be a note,

Here's your fucking note.

Fuck you.

Where were you?

I needed someone,

Just one, just one person,

I had no one.

I'm cursing you as I bleed out.

Fuck you.

Fuck a funeral, don't bother coming,

Why did it take my death for you to be present?

On my birthday you weren't ever present,

Why should my death day be different?

Be consistent with your energy,

Might as well have been an enemy.

How many times did I reach out?

How many times did I ask for help?

How many times did you see me cry?

How many times did I say I needed you?

Check your messages and count it up

Tell me how many times.

How many times was I there for you?

Even when it was inconvenient,

Even when I was in pain,

Even when there was rain,

I showed up.

I showed up every time,

Why didn't you show up for me?

Don't show up to this funeral.

There shouldn't be a funeral,

I wish a nigga would,

Put me in a casket made of wood.

Just burn me, burn it all,

Burn the notebooks filled with silent screams,

Burn all my hopes and dreams,

Burn them with me,

I'll take it all with me,

For my eyes only, it's wasted on you,

Fuck you.

Burn me like my anger burns,

I've never had more rage,

Bird trapped in a cage,

With nowhere to go,

Always flying solo,

Solo sin nadie,

Solo con nada,

El que no nada se ahoga,

Ya me canse y llegó la hora.

I'm tired of letting you people in,

Why are my tears seen as a sin?

Every shoulder to cry on,

Ends up pushing me away,

Nobody is ever here to stay,

Why is it always this way?

I struggle every fucking day.

I'm tired of climbing out the hole,

I feel the pain deep in my soul,

I celebrate every victory on my own,

I deal with every defeat alone,

I have a heart made of stone,

I hope you can hear my tone,

Fuck you.

Cremate me and turn me to ash,

Scatter me wherever I don't give a damn,

Don't bother holding on to the urn,

My only request is that you let me burn,

Just scatter the ashes to the sea,

Don't bother with a funeral for all the fake fucks to see,

"Why so harsh?" the family will say,

Well why show up only on this day?

You've been gone so long I forgot you existed,

You're only at the service because you insisted,

Cry and lament but it's all just for show,

I'm dead now so how would I know?

How would I hear of your little speeches?

In life you were just leeches,

Don't waste your breath on a speech,

I'm beyond earshot, way out of reach.

Why couldn't you say what you wanted while I was alive?

If you'd said it to my face maybe I would still be alive.

So I don't wanna hear it,

I can't even if I wanted to,

But you can read this,

Read it loud and clear,

Fuck you.

I'm dead and I'm gone,

Don't post pics and put on a front,

It's fake and it's a stunt,

Every cry for help was ignored,

I held on and kept the pain stored,

Til I couldn't hold it anymore,

My heart grew too sore.

I granted Myself sweet release,

I made the thoughts cease,

Now I'm at peace,

Enjoy my final piece

Of mind and final words,

To the real ones I say goodbye,

To the rest as I go to rest I say,

Fuck you.

STUNTED GROWTH

How can I grow when you stunt my growth?

How can I fly away when you clip my wings?

You want me to have what's mine,

But then you turn around and take it?

You say you want me on my own two feet,

But you're asking for an arm and a leg?

When I get out again I can't ever come back,

Because if I do I know you'll make it harder.

INSATIABLE

I'm afraid to get what I want,

'Cause once I got it I know,

It won't be enough.

Don't matter how long I've wanted it,

Once it's mine I'll have my eyes fixed on,

The next thing.

Then I'll realize the emptiness of it all,

The things I wanted don't make me happy,

It's all to fill a void that I can't close

With new clothes.

A PENNY FOR YOUR THOUGHTS

All the ideas that you called moronic,

Will be the same things that make me iconic.

BUSY BEE (BUZZY MIND)

We're not a hive but we are of one mind,

Talking about me and myself and I,

Of course, thoughts of death buzz

Loud in my head and it's because,

I'm alone and nothing can help me,

I use music to drown out those thoughts

That flood my mind,

A temporary reprieve,

Recess but I don't think it'll work forever.

I don't care enough to rhyme anymore,

I don't care about the time anymore,

I wondered this past week what

Would give out first,

My mind or my body?

I almost wanted something terminal

To just get it over with.

The human experience sucks,

Being alive is overrated.

THIS MOMENT, TODAY

I could have died yesterday,

I cried yesterday,

But here I am today,

And I'm glad.

I was sad,

It may return tomorrow,

That lingering sorrow,

Might need to borrow.

But today I'm here with you,

You're glad I'm here too.

It's just me and you,

Today's not so bad.

Yesterday I shed a tear,

Today I shed another tear,

Because I almost wasn't here.

I'd be sad if I missed out.

This is a truth I don't doubt,

A truth I can admit,

I'm glad I didn't forfeit,

This moment was worth it.

Thank you for today,

I'll make it to tomorrow.

Part Three

Love That Never Was

Introduction

I challenged myself to write some love poems. Whenever someone hears that I'm a poet, they assume I've written about love. I never really do. I haven't had a consistent muse about whom to write love poems. However, as I said, I challenged myself, and here we are. I wrote enough for a short section.

The poem "Black on Black" actually started as a joke. I was texting a friend of mine at the time and pretending to flirt with her. I started by sending a couple of lines. She liked it and encouraged me to send more, so I did. I wrote a few more lines; then I sat down and wrote out the entire poem.

I first wrote it as a song, actually. I was inspired by MF DOOM's lyrical style a bit, so there's actually a recording of my rapping this song over MF DOOM's instrumental beat "Fenugreek." That was just done for fun; I don't claim to be a rapper (I didn't say it was good). I never posted it anywhere, and I don't have the rights to publish that anyway. So it will not be released; you'll just have to imagine it. Perhaps someday, I will record it as a real song.

LOVE ON SIGHT

I had a love at first sight, shit,

But it started online,

Saw her in person,

Turned to love on-site, shit.

BLACK ON BLACK

Black on Black, it's a crime you can't see me.

Got my name tatted on you like graffiti; niggas hatin' 'cause they wanna be me.

I want all your attention; I guess I'm greedy.

Gotchu iced out even tho you ain't Saweetie.

It don't matter 'cause you still my sweetie.

I could tell you to stay tonight, but don't wanna be needy.

I said I'm old school, but I ain't got a CD

Player, and that's my name in this game,

you know, right now on the come-up before I hit fame.

It's a game, and she the dame of my choosing;

when she come around, I know I ain't losin'.

She asks me if I'm all in or all out.

Summer just started; I don't wanna tap out,

don't want what we got to stop and stall out.

Cause if shit go nuclear, how do I deal with the fallout?

This just one track about my hot-boy summer.

If you leave me right now, then it'll be a bummer.

I remember Armin[14], put my arm in 'cause I'm with it to the end,

not a nigga more faithful than that Eldian[15] friend.

Yeah, I got options, but this ain't pretend.

I'm the MVP; no other can contend.

If we fall apart now, it'll be colossal,

Fifty years later, lookin' back at old pics like a fossil.

I'm not a mutant, so I can't be your X-Man.

We stick together; yeah, that be the best plan.

Don't take these to be words from an imposter

Just because I got a summer roster.

Got my guard up around my heart like it's armor;

don't worry, girl; I'll cool down soon. Stick around. I'm a charmer.

---

[14]Armin is the name of a character from my favorite anime, *Attack On Titan*.
[15]Armin is part of a race of people called "Eldians."

PLUTO

I don't know why we keep each other around.

We're too far now to really be aware of each other,

But close enough to maintain the gravitational pull.

Just a little further away and we won't be connected.

I wanna get high and spend a day on Pluto.

Time is slower there, six earth days to one on Pluto.

Give me time; give me more time to work on myself.

Give me more time in the day and more time at night.

THE CULTURE OF VULTURES

This culture of using each other and being insincere,

It makes me feel like I don't belong here.

In this world where nothing is true,

I just wanted it to be me and you.

THE GULP

We talk about heart breaks.

You know, the love aches,

But before the heart sinks

And you say, "Love stinks,"

Feels like OJ pulp.

It's the gulp.

"We need to talk."

gulp

Now I can't walk.

Time freezes.

Heart seizes.

No sudden sneezes,

Nothing eases

The feeling that hits

When love's callin' it quits.

GROWING APART

I just wanna see you smile.

Won't you please stay a while?

We used to thirst for each other;

Now my phone stays dry as hell.

Used to talk every day,

Now you don't even say hey.

We always been far, but it never felt that way.

Don't leave me right now; please stay.

No texting me back, then all of a sudden,

You flood me with texts of all I did wrong,

Things you never told me before, and the language is strong.

Our love started online, and you stay on my mind.

I wanna feel your touch, so I stay on my grind

So we can get together and be together,

For better or worse, no matter the weather.

I read what you wrote, and I hear your voice.

If I did something wrong, it wasn't by choice;

I swear I'll do better; I'll do my part.

If you leave me right now, you leave with my heart.

THE INCONVENIENCE OF LOVE

We made love.

We made plans.

We made memories.

We got busy.

We couldn't make time.

SNAPE

I love you, but it's a love I'll never show.

I love you, but it's a love you'll never know.

It was love at first sight, but it was one-sided,

Unreciprocated, but I'm glad our paths collided.

I'll love you from afar.

You're a shining star,

My guiding light in the night sky.

I'm the owl, and I'll continue to fly

Solo because no one compares to you.

I've tried before, so I know it's true.

There are a million stars out in space,

But none are as beautiful as your face.

A love that doesn't bind could sever us,

So I shall take a page from Severus.[16]

I love you more than words can say.

I vow as your friend, for now and always,

I can only express my love in this rhyme.

---

[16]Severus Snape is a character from *Harry Potter*. He was in love with his childhood friend, Harry's mother, Lily, but she ended up with someone else. He loved her from afar for many years.

In the end, I'll say, "Yes, after all this time."[17]

DUMB SON

Wrote she redrum,

Wow that sounds fuckin dumb,

Just like you boy what a chum,

Talked to her twice and made her cum,

Thought we'd be stuck together like gum,

I want it all I don't want some,

Tally it up and I'll tell you the sum,

Now she's gone and not even a crumb,

Sitting here like a fuckin bum,

Fuck it man hand me the rum.

Said I wouldn't get played again,

But here I am once again

ONE MORE (TASTE OF YOUR LOVIN')

Doo Wop vibes

Ooooooh ooooooooooh

Ooooooooooh, ooooooh, oooooh,

I just want one more,

One more taste of your lovin,

I just want one more,

One more moment one more,

One more taste of your skin,

Seeing your grin.

One more taste of your lips,

(Just one more kiss)

Baby it's goodbye ,

I just want one more,

Hand on your chin,

Taste of your skin,

Pull back and I see you grin,

Is it a sin?

Don't wanna come in I know we're through,

But I still love you,

So I want one more taste of your lovin,

Call it closure,

Call it over,

Sealed with a kiss,

I just want one more taste of your lovin,

The last bit of love we got left for each other,

Before we part ways and share our skin with another,

At this moment we're still lovers,

Just one more kiss,

One more moment,

One more taste of your lovin.

TO THE HOT MELANIN MAMI

Every tortured artist needs a muse,

Whatever role you want me to play you choose,

I'm hooked to you but I know you won't abuse,

If I think about you too hard I'll blow a fuse.

You shine so bright,

there's no hiding your light,

Drunk in love that's unrequited,

I don't give a fuck I'm not trynna fight it.

I'm stuck to you like to you like the moon is to earth,

Caught in your field at a distance cause I know your worth,

More than words can say,

I'll tell you every single day.

You're the loveliest sight to behold,

It'll be that way til we grow old,

I don't care if these words are bold,

You need to be told.

You astonish me everytime I see you,

Every mortal man should feel this way too,

Your beauty is unmatched inside and out,

I'm spitting these rhymes because I have no doubt.

I speak the truth so I say it with ease,

Just be my muse is all I ask baby please,

While neither of us has a lover,

You're my queen and I'm the other.

The one who sings praises of you each day,

I wouldn't have it any other way,

Words aren't enough to grasp how I feel,

I'm drunk but the emotions are real.

DEAR RUBY

Ruby, Ruby!

You shine so bright!

Ruby, Ruby!

You not very bright.

Ruby, Ruby!

Why so mean?

Ruby, Ruby!

Jewel of a queen.

Ruby, Ruby!

Mother of many.

Ruby, Ruby!

Men are aplenty.

Ruby, Ruby!

Gilded, not gold.

Ruby, Ruby!

You're gettin' old.

Ruby, Ruby!

You stay jammin'.

Ruby, Ruby!

You stay slammin'.

Ruby, Ruby!

Got an itch.

Ruby, Ruby!

You a bitch.

Ruby, Ruby!

Now you mad at me.

Ruby, Ruby!

I'll keep it PG.

Ruby, Ruby!

Left the kids alone.

Ruby, Ruby!

Your truth is shown.

Ruby, Ruby!

Got me out in these streets.

Ruby, Ruby!

Enjoy your new sheets.

Ruby, Ruby!

Got a new blouse.

Ruby, Ruby!

Got a new house.

Ruby, Ruby!

In your golden years.

Ruby, Ruby!

Holdin onto your fears.

Ruby, Ruby!

We'll bury you here.

Ruby, Ruby!

I won't shed a tear.

NO NUT NOVEMBER

Let's keep it real,

This how I feel.

It be that post nut clarity,

Missing you is a rarity.

Giving a fuck that's my charity,

Not real love, just a parody.

WON'T BE

R&B vibes

Cause now you broke my heart and this all fell apart and you coming back saying baby let's start

Over again why pretend and hide feelings like they ain't still there?

So why did you act like you ain't care?

Can't go back to how it used to be,

Somethings break that you can't put together,

Time heals wounds but the scar still there,

What we had can never be again,

Last time really was the end,

You can't come back

Cause now it won't be, won't be, won't be like it used to be.

Cause now it won't be can't be can't you see just set me free

Cause now it won't be, won't be, won't be like it used to be.

Cause now it won't be can't be can't you see just set me free

I'm not mad I still wish you the best,

Can't front like I don't miss the past,

I saw you in my future but just like the seasons these feelings

weren't meant to last,

I gambled once, this time ima let it pass,

Cause now it won't be, won't be, won't be like it used to be.

Cause now it won't be can't be can't you see just set me free,

Just let me be.

THE VOW (TO MY BELOVED)

I don't know you yet but this is what I wanted to say in
advance:

I love you, my Black Queen.

I want to treat you like royalty, the way you deserve.

I want to make up for the way the world has treated you.

I'm unsure of so many things but I'm certain of my love for
you.

You may not know what the future holds but know that I'll
hold you.

I never want to give you a reason to doubt my love

I'll remind you everyday in every way

Breakfast in bed with a side of head,

Kisses and dick whenever you wish,

I'll help you wash your hair,

Let's do skin care,

Get our nails done together and I'll pay,

Massages every night after a long day,

I have so much love to give and I wanna give it all to you

I love you so much and if you're reading this it means you

were worth the wait,

I only plan to read this to my wife,

The one with whom I'll spend my life.

INSPIRATIONS

In this section I will explain my inspiration for writing some of my poems. I'll try to be brief so as to not explain the poem itself. I won't be explaining all of them!

THE EXILED CHILD/THE EXILED CHILD II

I wrote this poem right after I finished watching *Roots*. I was deeply moved at the end when Alex Haley found the tribe in Africa where his ancestor Kunta Kinte was from. Most of us in the diaspora don't know where we are from or what our original last name was. I wanted to write a poem about that lack of original identity. Don't get it twisted, I know we have a culture that we created in our new nations with traces of our roots in them. All of us have heavily influenced the culture in the countries we found ourselves in.

Anyway, in this poem, I'm addressing Mother Africa as an exiled child, I'm writing to her about what's happened to us since we were taken.

BLESSED ASSURANCE

This poem is directed towards Father God. I wrote this when I began to have serious doubts about my Christian faith. Essentially this became the poem that signified my break from Christianity. The reasons listed here aren't the only reason I stopped believing, but they were definitely major grievances I had with God directly.

I AM AT WAR

All I can say is this was all a true story. I wasn't really using metaphors here, no need when the reality was so unbelievable. I was in middle school when Obama won the election the first time, you wouldn't believe how many white children were angry at me because he won. They were angry because he was Black and for no other reason. I'm sure a lot of other Black people can relate to that experience.

I really did see a white man in full Klan robes riding his bike down the main business highway in Angleton the day Trump won the election. He was wearing the black robes and making the white power sign with his hands on his bike.

DEATH PARADE

I was inspired by Billie Holiday's "Strange Fruit." Written by Abel Meeropol under the pseudonym Lewis Allan and performed by Holiday. The lynching that inspired this poem the most was that of Jesse Washington here in Texas in 1916. I was appalled at how drawn out his lynching was. Keeping his murder and many others in mind along with what Holiday suffered for performing her song, I started to pen the poem.

I AM SERIES (I-IV)

When God first speaks to Moses in the book of Exodus, he presents himself as "I Am." I'm not religious anymore as I've said, but I like the power in the statement. It's simple yet bold, it says a lot without saying a lot. The series focuses on the idea that the gods did not create humanity, humanity created the gods. Humans gave the gods all the power that they themselves hold within.

I AM II was inspired by the Boondocks theme song by Asheru. The theme song always struck me as a powerful affirmation and I wanted to make something similar to that. The other element to that was the statement, "I am Malcolm X!" but instead I used my own activist name.

WHERE ARE YOUR PAPERS?

This is one I'm actually going to explain a bit because nobody seems to get it. The question is asked to Black people of course, during slavery and then after the Civil War during the sharecropping days. Then the question is repeated three times before switching to Spanish. The first meaning behind the repetition is to signify the passage of time. The second meaning is like repeating a question that the other person can't understand. The repetition is meant to be read slower each time before switching to Spanish. The reader is to infer that the same question is being asked to an immigrant now,

"Where are your papers?"

When we speak of Latinx immigrants or Latinx people in general, people tend to always forget that Afro Latinx people exist. Just wanted to throw that reminder out there.

GREAT-GREAT-GREAT-GRANDMOMMA TRAUMA

I wrote this about my real ancestor, I do not know her name, I only know of her son, Henry.

THE OWL IN THE OLD OAK TREE (IMITATION OF MEDITATION XVII)

The story is mostly fictional/metaphorical but it is based on a real oak tree in the center of Houston where at least two Black men were lynched.

THE ORCA: BLACK & WHITE

I wrote this about Shamu.

WONDER WOMAN

All of us look up to somebody whether it's a parent, politician, historical figure, etc. You don't truly know them though, we make assumptions about people we've never met in person. Sometimes our heroes disappoint us.

DANTE TRILOGY

The Divine Comedy by Dante Alighieri inspired this series. I wanted to write my own version of it, much shorter of course. Both Dantes travel through hell, purgatory and heaven.

THE BALLOT/THE BULLET

Listen to Malcolm X's 1964 speech "The Ballot or the Bullet." That was the direct inspiration.

THE ABUSE

No Mom and Dad, I'm not saying I smoke marijuana. Slang for marijuana is Mary Jane, I wanted to write about a toxic/abusive relationship with a double meaning. Using drugs is called "drug abuse" and while I don't believe that drugs such as Mary Jane are bad, I still wanted to use the name for this purpose. It's all a double entendre.

THE DEATH NOTE II

I know this poem is very raw and angry. I wanted to show that suicidal, depressed people are not simply "sad." Depression is more than sadness and only people with depression truly understand the many moods and emotions that come with it. I had addressed the emptiness in previous poems. I wanted to express the anger here, the frustration caused by the pits of loneliness and mental illness. I honestly debated deleting this poem from the manuscript, but again, I wanted to demonstrate a different side of suicide.

THE X-COMMUNICATED

(Bullet Points)

1. America is an empire

2. Voting is merely the illusion of choice, a false hope for change

3. There is nowhere to run from the empire

4. There are no good presidents under an evil empire

5. The Diaspora wars must end, the only way to win is to come together

6. Peaceful protests and unorganized riots are both ineffective

7. We must create the change we want to see, that means no more waiting for politicians and corporations to make those changes

8. There is no time to wait, earth is dying. We must act now

9. Those in power will not willingly give up their privilege, it must be taken by force.

10. Ending capitalism will not end racism, misogyny, homophobia, etc.

11. Dismantling the American empire won't be enough to end white supremacy; white supremacy is all over the world. The European powers are just as corrupt

12. Christianity has become a tool for white supremacist ideology, it is unrecognizable from its original roots 2000 years ago.

13. All the wealth and progress that Europe and America boasts comes from what they've stolen from the Global South

14. Individual power is not enough, we need the power of the collective, the masses to make a change and the empire knows this which is why they keep us divided

15. Intersectionality matters and must be considered in every fight for liberation. ALL Black lives matter, not just the lives of straight cis-gender Black men.